Dazzling
Design

STEWART, TABORI & CHANG | NEW YORK

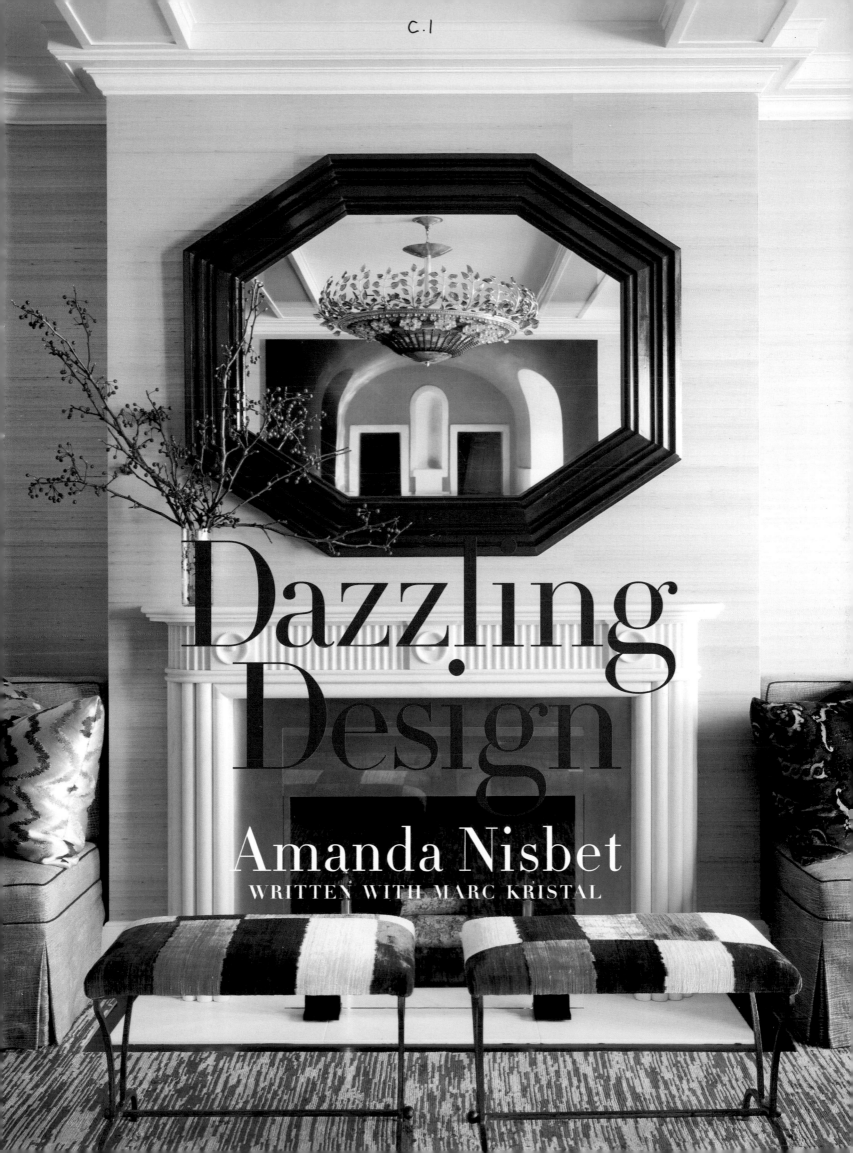

Dazzling Design

Amanda Nisbet
WRITTEN WITH MARC KRISTAL

To my parents, Joe and Susan Travers, my sister, Francesca, my husband, Chip, and my children, Alannah and Travers. With my deepest love and affection I dedicate this book to you.
"Dum Vivimus Vivamus"

Introduction

When I think about my years as an interior designer, I'm reminded of Dorothy's observation in *The Wizard of Oz*—that if you want to find your heart's desire, the place to look is your own backyard. I say this because there was a time when I believed that what I *really* wanted to be was an actress—despite a life that, in so many ways, prepared me for the profession I have today.

I come from an aesthetically minded family that immersed me, virtually from the start, in the decorative and fine arts. Mum would move furniture for therapy, Dad was a frustrated architect, and they took great pleasure in creating beautiful homes together. We also traveled a great deal, mostly through Europe (our home base was Montreal), and I wasn't a child who had to be dragged to museums: the Louvre, Uffizi, Victoria and Albert—I loved them all.

In college, I majored in both art history and Italian,—spending a year studying in Florence because I wanted to focus on the Renaissance and had realized that I wouldn't be able to grasp it properly without a full understanding of the language. To me, the historical, cultural, and political environments that produced some of the supreme artistic achievements of Western civilization were as important as the works themselves; learning about them in the city where the Renaissance began greatly broadened and refined my sensibilities.

After graduation, I had the best job imaginable, as a cataloger at Christie's auction house in New York. I started out in the Impressionist painting department, and as I researched a picture's provenance and history, the process reinforced what I had discovered in Florence: that no object can be entirely divorced from its context. From paintings, I moved on to the jewelry department; working with gemstones and their settings, I received an unexpected immersion in color. Studying opacity, luster, brilliance, and hue had a transforming effect on my eye.

When I returned to Canada, I again got lucky and was hired to work with the director of design and display at Ogilvy's, a fine Montreal department store, where I was responsible for creating

My inspirations for a room I designed for the Kips Bay Show House in Manhattan—you can see it on pages 150–59—included a coral necklace that gave me my primary color, fabric swatches that supported it, and a saucy detail from a canvas by Fragonard that influenced the room's spirit.

window displays and floor arrangements. This proved to be a fantastic on-the-job education in design; it taught me how to create eye-catching tableaux, to stay light-spirited, and not to be afraid to take chances (or even be a little outrageous).

So what did I do with all this? I got married, moved back to Manhattan, and started making the rounds as an actress—I knew that if I didn't give it a try, I'd always regret it. Two years later, with one child and a second on the way, I stopped. I loved the work, but the unreliability of the actor's life simply wasn't for me, especially with a family to care for. I did, however, learn an important decorating lesson from the relationship between the actor and the set. I discovered that stage design isn't just about creating pretty pictures, but rather about building a space where things can happen between the players, one that supports and encourages the life unfolding within it—something that is equally indispensable in a residential interior.

I'm not sure quite when, but at some point during my acting life I began helping friends design their homes. Usually the projects were small, and no one had much money. But it brought me back to my own backyard, and I was reminded how much I loved and missed design. I also realized something else: that it gave me great pleasure to make people happy, to see their joy at discovering what a difference a nice home can make in one's life. So, having found my way back to my heart's desire, I hung out a shingle and went to work—and almost fifteen years and nearly a hundred projects later, I've never had a moment's regret.

While I have always worked instinctively, there are certain fundamentals upon which my approach is based. Uppermost is the idea of the vitalizing juxtaposition—of styles, colors, periods, and textures—that gives a room an agreeable tension. My art history studies and my work at Christie's taught me that no object is an island unto itself, and it's my job—as well as my pleasure—to look at a collection of seemingly disparate elements and uncover a larger order that will be exciting and unexpected.

Closely connected to this is my belief that part of that mix—a big part—should come from my clients. Many decorators don't want clients to display family photos or include personal mementos in "correct" interiors. I couldn't disagree more—I think it's essential to embrace the past as well as the present, to incorporate not only treasures you've inherited but also things you've found yourself. They're all part of what gives soul and individuality to my work—and they make the difference between rooms that merely reflect a decorator's grand plan and ones that look like I've brought out the best in *you*.

Above all, I am certain that interiors can and should have bits of wit and whimsy about them, things that serve to throw them slightly off balance. Rooms that are too serious, or too perfect, don't encourage you to relax and have fun. And after all, what else is a home for?

My year in Florence was aesthetically formative in large part because the Italians, more than any people I've met, take great joy in the beauty of life. That may be the most important of all the lessons I've learned. The creative process is incredibly rewarding, but what keeps me coming back—it may sound like a cliché, but it's the truth—is making people happy by shaping a cornucopia of pleasures in which my clients can cultivate the art of living.

That is my heart's desire, and it is my pleasure to share it here.

Mila Corsini Bland

Bold Beginnings

Find the right opening gesture—one that perfectly captures a design's theme— and everything else will flow from it

Where to begin? If you've ever engaged in any kind of creative endeavor, you know just how challenging—or maddening—that question can be. I'm never entirely at sea: I start by speaking with my clients—for hours, sometimes days—about their dreams of how they want to live. And I know that in most instances I'm going to design the living room first, because it's the nexus of the home, the aesthetic point of reference for all the other spaces. But to *truly* get under way, I have to find the one thing—the perfect object, fabric, color, or gesture—that encapsulates everything about a client's personality and desires, and serves as the inspiration from which all my subsequent decisions will flow. It can take a while—sometimes a *long* while. But once I discover what I'm looking for, I know I've launched the ship of the design on the right course.

In my own New York apartment, the perfect inspiration proved to be the bright-orange boiled wool from which I made the living room curtains. The reason? I'm from Canada—and up north, we always want to come inside, sit by the fire, and get cozy. Boiled wool has a wonderfully nubby texture—just the sort of scrumptious material you'd want to wrap yourself in to feel warm and protected. As soon as I had it in my hands, it spoke to me of home.

I loved that it was orange, too, which is not only a happy color (it was Frank Sinatra's favorite) but also an approachable one. If I'd done my curtains in a silk vermillion, let's say, the living room might have felt a bit intimidating—I'd always somehow have to be *up* for how elegantly the room was dressed. In every room, but especially in the space where I entertain, I want people to feel relaxed and welcome, and orange is a good color in that way—inclusive.

Of course, it's counterintuitive to make curtains out of what is tantamount to your security blanket, and when I sent the fabric to my workshop, my seamstress called to say, "They'll be too heavy—you're breaking the rules." Fortunately, after fifteen years of practice, I've learned which rules you can break—and those cozy, bright curtains set the perfect tone for my entire home.

PREVIOUS PAGES: Having been an actress, I have great respect for supporting players—and with bright orange curtains singing the lead role in my living room, quieter colors provide a soothing chorus. OPPOSITE: A pair of palm trees from the estate of Evangeline Bruce stands before a spirited impressionistic view of Venice by Bob Kane.

The layering of
multiple textures—
linen, wool, felt, and
velvet—all in the
same family of
neutral colors cre-
ates a backdrop
that's calming
without subtracting
depth or dimension.

Even if they're more quietly on display, details form an important layer— they enhance, support, and complete a room's design

In the living room, unusual objects include a giltwood "nut" (OPPOSITE) that I placed atop a Macassar table. Brass nail heads (BELOW, LEFT AND RIGHT) outlining different furnishings add a contrasting vitality to the soft and welcoming upholstery. An elegant Georgian armchair (LEFT), its mahogany frame finished with beautifully carved details, is upholstered in an unexpectedly casual velvet corduroy.

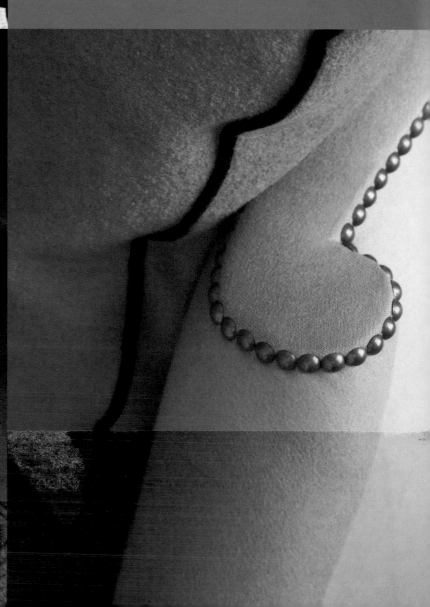

I want rooms to look considered but not overly "decorated," as though I'd gone to a show-room, purchased a matched suite of fancy furnishings, and airlifted it into a client's living room. So I try to create varied, salon-style spaces that look as though they'd been put together over time, out of a myriad of favorite finds unified by a single sensibility.

Though it's said that you should never do it, "Mess with perfection" is one of my mantras. And for good reason: When rooms are too perfect, they can be a bit lifeless. My solution is to completely finish a space, then add an element that throws it a bit off balance. Rather than spoiling the effect, this gesture creates a special frisson that makes a room exciting and a design that's genuinely timeless.

A good example can be found in the tableau I constructed beside the fireplace in my living room. It features objects both acquired and inherited: a beautifully patinated neoclassical console from the estate of the legendary Washington grande dame Evangeline Bruce, on which I arranged favorite books and my grandfather's engraved silver boxes beneath a pair of prints I got from my parents. It's a layered mélange that captures the essence of my approach: a casual-seeming—but carefully considered—collage of color, texture, and pattern.

But it felt a little too serious, too predictable—so I tucked a pair of Lucite stools of my own design, crowned with purple-velvet-covered cushions, beneath Mrs. Bruce's marble-topped antique. Now I've got the luminosity of Lucite, the roughness of aged wood, the sparkle of the silver against the matte of the prints—and the unexpected cheek of those bright purple pillows to make it all more vital.

I should add that though I'm pleased with this vignette, it's a mistake to let objects get too comfortable in their places. I'm constantly changing artworks and moving accessories around the house; putting things in different locations gives them new lives—you see them in a new way, and experience the space with a fresh perspective. Think of how your friends come over and always throw themselves into the same pieces of furniture. If you move them around, the people remain the same but the dynamic changes. The same thing happens when you rearrange a room's components.

OPPOSITE: In a corner of my living room, a number of elements of varying quality, seriousness, and provenance—everything from artworks I "borrowed" from my parents to an important neoclassical table to a pair of Lucite stools of my own design— form a thoughtfully arranged but relaxed tableau. Flowers (above) complete the picture.

I like to combine finishes that play off each
the luminosity of a mirror and the

other — the matte of white plaster supporting
shine of nickel against rough limestone

My living room is anchored at one end by a fireplace with an oval-shaped mirror above the mantelpiece, and on the other by a superb William Yeoward armoire (in which I hide the television). Together they create a pleasurable balance that avoids strict symmetry.

In a modern building, the challenge is all about bringing forth the best in the spaces— while also neutralizing the negatives

I love contemporary architecture, both aesthetically and for its compatibility with the way we all like to live, but it can give a residence a bit of a hard edge. Similarly, few things are more dynamic than the light, sweep, and sheer spectacle afforded by floor-to-ceiling glass (especially after dark, when a city becomes a lovely, twinkly wonderland)—but an urban view can be visually noisy and occasionally unsettling. My task, in this Manhattan living room for a family of six, was to embrace the pleasures of the setting and the architecture while protecting the residents from the aggressive aspects of both—by creating a room that would be as calm and comfortable as it was urbane.

Layering plays a big part in my work, and it was especially important here: First, patterned rattan scrims, then curtains stitched from a yellow-and-beige ikat, soften the expanses of glass, and textured linen on the walls banishes the ubiquitous chill of drywall. I also paid close attention to the interior architecture, arranging the room's horizontal and vertical elements—the low line of the sofas, the tall, symmetrically placed lamps—to gently lay an organizing grid over the urban chaos outside the windows.

A high comfort quotient was established by the upholstered pieces and cozy carpet, but I also zoned the room to make it more inviting and user-friendly. To avoid "floating" the sofas—which can make you feel uncomfortably on display—I anchored them in front of the windows (while still maintaining communication with the views). And it was important to make sure the room felt equally workable for a large group or a single individual, so I created furniture groupings of different sizes—I especially like the sculptural, stand-alone leather chaise that lets you enjoy the action without having to participate in it.

Just to make sure things didn't get too serene, I introduced a repeating circle motif, elongating one into an oval coffee table and twisting others into biomorphic shapes—it gives the design unity but also vitality. And I used the opportunity afforded by my clients' request that I select artworks to add an elegant visual joke: A photographic diptych featuring the crowded steps of the Metropolitan Museum, by the Korean artist Sangbin IM, brings the crazy, cacophonous city we've worked to hold in abeyance right back into the room. That kind of gesture—which suggests that, however elegant your home, you don't take yourself too seriously—is what gives a room panache.

This undulating cantilevered side table reminded me of a wave. As its placement between two taller armchairs required a bit of height, I topped the table with a contrastingly angular brass sculpture—one that can be reshaped with a few twists and turns.

Horizontals, verticals, layers, and forms create a domino effect in design—take away even one element and they all fall down

Introducing a repeating circle motif at once vitalizes the design and gives it unity

The living room's repeating circular motif—which gives the space vitality as well as unity—appears in the circa 1940 Italian blown-glass balls (ABOVE RIGHT) and the powder-coated steel "Montreal" sconces of my own design (ABOVE LEFT). OPPOSITE: Sangbin IM's photographic diptych introduces New York's human cacophony into the otherwise soothing room.

High *Punch* Color

Using strong color can be a high-wire act, but if you can keep your balance, the effect is transformative

THE DEATH OF
ARTEMIO
CRUZ
Carlos
Fuentes

Greene on Capri · Shirley Hazzard

DORIS
KEARNS
GOODWIN

TEAM OF RIVALS
THE POLITICAL GENIUS OF ABRAHAM LINCOLN

GABRIEL GARCÍA MÁRQUEZ
ERÉNDIRA
Harper

The moment you tell me what your favorite color is—even if that's all you tell me—I can design your entire home. That's because I respond strongly, indeed intuitively, to color: to the immediate visceral responses it provokes, and to how different colors will work for different individuals. And as my own pea-green study demonstrates, I am not timid about my choices.

As much as I believe in continuity, I also think it's important to get something different from every space, to suit your varying needs and personalities (maybe it's the Sybil in me). I often suggest that clients set one room aside to serve as a cocoon, whether it's the dining room, the library, or, as in my case, the study. A cocoon is essential—it's the one place in the house where you don't have to have your game on. And while some might think a dark saturation of color would be oppressive, in fact the opposite is true: a total immersion in a single shade—provided it's the right one—produces a singular emotional experience: you're immediately swept up in a passionate embrace. Which is why such rooms can be the most welcoming, and consoling, of all.

Of course, using strong saturations of color requires the utmost discernment. As the idea is to create a specific mood, the technique is most appropriate to smaller spaces dedicated to introspection or intimate gatherings—it's less effective in a living room meant to accommodate a multitude of uses. Darker jewel tones lend themselves to total immersion more readily than lighter shades: boysenberry, aubergine, cerulean, cinnamon. But whatever the color, it has to be absolutely spot on: a millishade off, and the effect is lost. Indeed, when clients call and say, "Please help, I'm repainting the nursery—give me a standard off-the-shelf color," I politely, but firmly, refuse. If I don't see it on site, I can't guarantee the results—it's that precise an art.

PREVIOUS PAGES: Into my lustrous pea-green study, black-and-white photos of Mick Jagger, Yves Saint Laurent, and the iconic model Veruschka inject the flair of an exclusive Swinging Sixties London club.
OPPOSITE: Gold side tables are small in scale but big on glamour.

Patterns, pinstripes, and objects add layers and levity— and prevent you from disappearing into a color void

OPPOSITE: The high sheen of the glossily lacquered walls is counterbalanced by a wealth of texture. Like the leaf-patterned carpet, the ikat pillows (BELOW RIGHT) give the room a slight Orientalist flavor, while the tightly tailored gray pin-striped flannel (BELOW LEFT) accentuates the sharp profile of the chair.

Subtle variations in color
create vibrant surfaces
and a rich sense of depth

In this living room, silver lamé
stitched into the cotton drapes
creates undulations reminiscent of
water—lamé is a material not
ordinarily associated with elegance,
but here it is highly effective.

T here's architecture, and there's color—and then there's color that effectively functions as an architectural element by influencing the ways in which a room's tectonic properties are perceived. It can be difficult to pull off, but when the circumstances are appropriate, making the distinction between the two elements ambiguous imbues an interior with an unusual—and uniquely pleasurable—cohesion.

This living room, in a New York apartment possessed of what decorators like to call "good bones," has just the sort of strongly articulated structure that lends itself to color enhancement. The beamed ceiling, moldings, and door surrounds announce their presence and, indeed, the furnishings follow the architecture's lead: The bolts holding together the rectilinear coffee tables are clearly, deliberately expressed, and even the geometric rows of buttons on the tufted sofa and bench march in time to the room's rhythm.

For the dominant color, I selected a sapphire blue of particular depth and intensity. While it emphasizes the planar rigidity (in a positive sense) of the architecture—making the sofas and, to a degree, the carpet feel like built elements within the room—the particular dark radiance of the shade also seems to float in a dimension of its own, as though the color itself were hovering in space.

I also appreciate the thematic interplay between the sapphire sofa and the large-format photograph above it: a salon in a once-grand South American villa that has been devastated by a flood. It is a quietly severe artwork that encourages contemplation—and that blue, by intensifying the architecture's force and drawing one into the color's depths, contributes to the meditative mood.

To amplify the textural quality of the silver lamé curtains, I covered the walls in a silk-blend paper with pronounced striations. Banquettes upholstered in a woven silk-and-cotton fabric (overleaf) extend the effect to the furnishings.

The chandelier, with its mix of mercury-glass inserts and blue and clear glass decorative motifs, brings femininity and glamour into an otherwise angular, slightly severe space.

OPPOSITE: The placement of the antique mirror above the fireplace captures the reflection of both the chandelier and the photograph on the wall opposite—creating the impression that the fixture is suspended in the room pictured in the image. The softly sculpted plaster lamp (LEFT), custom crafted by Stephen Antonson, with whom I frequently collaborate, sits atop a side table by the artist and furniture designer Ingrid Donat. The stools (ABOVE RIGHT) were a serendipitous find: They include all the colors in the room—plus an extra jolt of purple and yellow.

50

My custom-designed black glass-and-brass dining tables, and the ivory ceiling lacquered to a high gloss, both reflect the light from a quartet of chandeliers, bringing sparkle to an already sexy room.

Just as the Greeks and Romans developed rules governing scale and proportion to create architectural masterworks, individuals as diverse as Leonardo da Vinci, Isaac Newton, Johann Wolfgang von Goethe, and Josef Albers have sought for centuries to formalize principles pertaining to the understanding of color. Most of us are broadly familiar, if only from art class, with some of these efforts, and have basic knowledge regarding primary, secondary, and complementary colors.

But color theory—which incorporates considerations of light, context, combination, medium, temperature, and countless other factors—is remarkably complex. So I'm grateful that, just as every designer has something that comes naturally, I have a reliably intuitive understanding of color. What I've found repeatedly is that the positive tension in my work derives from unexpected juxtapositions: forms and textures, periods and styles, colors most of all.

The dining room on the previous pages is finished in multiple shades of purple: There's boysenberry on the walls, a deep plum banquette, fuchsia dining chairs, lavender pillows. The diptych on the wall, however, is predominantly slate blue and yellow, colors found elsewhere in the apartment. The artwork disrupts the room's unity even as it creates connection. The result is something arresting: not one color or another, but an *effect*.

For that lesson, I'm indebted to my great inspiration, the painter Mark Rothko, and his sometimes outrageous, eye-scorching combinations. What Rothko was after was an experience. And an experience, I've discovered, is larger than the laws of color.

OPPOSITE: The deep navy blue of this smoking room makes it a cozy cocoon. I replicated the herringbone pattern of the floor in the custom-designed carpet, and its mix of caramel and faun coloring introduces a more feminine aspect while also adding warmth.

I'd already decided on the purple upholstery for the arm-chair and throw pillows when my clients and I came upon Marilyn Minter's photograph—which we liked not only for its provocative nature, but for the way the subject's lips and nails played off that purple.

A deep shade of blue migrates from place to place in this room, interspersed with warm moments of complementary caramel

The smoking room reflects my belief that layered textures give a room depth, interest, and, indeed, panache. The sofa pillows feature square velvet appliqués on a wool background; blue leather on the tufted sofa is as richly grained as corduroy; alternating squares and circles, in purple and blue, add an almost architectural articulation to the curtains and shades. My "Swank" nickel-and-shagreen sconces feature navy shades that help them dissolve into the walls. The bar, an appendage indispensable to any proper smoking room, is tucked neatly into a closet.

When we imagine an intimately scaled room bathed in a rich, dark hue, the adjectives that most readily come to mind are *glamorous, luxurious, sexy.* But going to the dark side, colorwise, may produce a more lighthearted experience. As this deep-blue home theater (installed in an awkward basement space) suggests, varying the ways in which dark colors are deployed can support a variety of functions and moods—not all of them serious.

Unlike my own study, the surfaces of which I painted a single lustrous green, the theater's walls are covered in a matte-finished, faux-shagreen paper featuring a pale vertical stripe—which, with the reflective silver-leafed ceiling, make the confining space feel taller and more voluminous. Though the materials are refined and invest the room with luminosity and luxury, using textured finishes and varying the shade subtly shifts the room's emotional temperature away from high glamour and toward an elegantly playful, Arabian Nights–style fantasia (made cozy by the wool carpet and ultrasuede banquettes).

That slightly tongue-in-cheek quality is entirely appropriate to a room that's used for entertainment, and I supported it with Moroccan-influenced pendant lanterns and quatrefoil mirrors. The colorful patterned pillows and carpet—and the pink piping on the banquettes—inject a dash of excitement without subtracting from the pleasurably enveloping blue.

Perhaps the theater isn't as chic and sexy—as grown-up—as my green room. But thanks to a rich infusion of color, a subterranean space that might otherwise have been piled with pet carriers and out-of-season sports equipment makes an enjoyable contribution to family life. Its movie-palace-in-miniature mystery enhances the children's video-watching experience—and the grown-ups can have cocktails down there without feeling like they're trapped in Disneyland.

OPPOSITE: For a media/family room that draws on multiple North African influences, I designed a Moroccan-style lantern that located the color element—a painted steel candelabrum—within a simple brass-and-glass enclosure. The Mylar pouf isn't exactly indigenous, but it is fun.

Sometimes a room's accent color can be supplied by a material—as with the nickel elements in this black office

OPPOSITE: To turn what had been a small, undistinguished white room into this chic, sexy office, I relied on bold materials: leather and dark wood paired with nickel trim and a black hide carpet.

Patterns introduce subtle variations into color and bring surfaces to life— including speckled mercury glass, perforated metal shades, and trim rivets

OPPOSITE: The custom horsehair rug in this office owes a debt to the black-on-black canvases of Ad Reinhardt. A chair covered in mustard-yellow velvet, paired with a vintage 1960s three-arm floor lamp, sits before an olive-green faux-lizard wallpaper chosen for the dimension it gives the room. I chose the vintage mercury and clear-glass pendant, both for its relationship to the casework's nickel accents and for the soft glow with which it infuses the space. And to make sure all that black and green doesn't become too oppressive, the ceiling was lacquered in an acidic yellow.

Everyone gravitates to blue at the beach, but for this family room in a house by the sea, I wanted to go in an unexpected direction—a rich fiddlehead green. The half-dozen wall sconces, by the designer David Weeks, I painted different colors and hung haphazardly, to create an artful arrangement that also provides soft ambient light. The eggshell-shaped chairs are, appropriately, for the family's hatchlings: the kids.

As a rule, people avoid strong color for fear of making a mistake. However, in my experience (and though it may seem counterintuitive) it's the white spaces that require the most bravery. To understand why, think of a woman dressed entirely in shades of white: a yummy cashmere sweater, slacks of crisp gabardine, a wool jacket with an elegant drape—everything has to be impeccable (her figure included). So it is with a white room. You can't conceal the architecture's imperfections—or the details of a design scheme. With nowhere to hide, every aesthetic choice must be that much more carefully considered.

Accordingly, the layering of whites requires a special attention to texture and finish. In this beach-house bedroom—typically bathed in beautiful sunlight—that meant combining a nubby carpet with the low luster of a patent-leather bench, setting a glossily lacquered chest of drawers against a matte-painted wall, and covering crisp cotton sheets with a white-on-white vermicelli-quilted bedspread. The mix of different materials and finishes, all so close in hue, imbues the room with the kind of subtly cheerful vitality that belongs to white alone.

Of course, it goes without saying that white isn't just white, all whites don't play well with one another, and pairing the wrong white with a particular color can inflect it with a tinge akin to an unhealthy pallor. To showcase the tart turquoise accents in this bedroom, I had to find whites that would not only work collectively, but would also warm up the color without going too yellow; though we don't ordinarily see it as such, white is in fact a complementary color.

My clients typically think of me as a colorist, and they're sometimes surprised when I suggest a white palette. I point out that if you revolve a color wheel at a high speed, you'll get a white blur—white is the *presence* of all color, not its absence. Besides, as every woman who dares to venture out in a white ensemble knows: no guts, no glory.

I enlivened this crisp, white beach-house bedroom with a single shade of turquoise, deployed in multiple ways—as a bold zigzag on the curtains, in quieter patterns on the banquette pillows, and as a solid tone on the stool cushions and accessories.

I try to design summer houses so that they'll be enjoyable in all seasons. The inviting freshness of this guest room, finished in an unusual combination of orange and pink, brings cheer even in the dead of winter.

Multidirectional beadboard with a glossy finish gives white an unexpected depth—and forms a lively backdrop for bold colors in vivid motion

Three nested powder-coated steel tables, in the sitting area of an attic bedroom at a beach house, complement the color of the wraparound sofa and, as the room's occupant is a college boy, can stand up to a beating.

In this potentially awkward attic room, in which the ceiling is lower than it appears, I created the illusion of greater height by orienting the wallboards vertically, then brought in a textural sense by running them horizontally on the sloped ceiling. A luminous white semigloss keeps the mood crisp and fresh.

A crisp graphic treatment makes a traditional trio of colors feel fresh and contemporary

A red, white, and navy color scheme always appeals, and it remains an especially welcome treatment in a beach house. Wide horizontal red and blue stripes on the headboard and window shades, and narrower vertical pinstripes for the bed skirt, give the room an elegant spin.

LEROY GRANNIS

TASCHEN

Soothing Style

There are many ways to make a room into a comforting cocoon—and none of them need be predictable

"Soothing" has to be one of the more misunderstood design concepts. There are two great clichés associated with it: minimalist—aka "Zen," which seems to have as many meanings as there are people—and monochrome. My own interpretation is simple: A soothing design includes the particular elements that make a person feel soothed—and everyone is different.

Some people—like those for whom I designed this urbane bedroom—are soothed by glamour. True, the palette is neutral, and the decoration is pared to a minimum. Yet the simple, architectural canopy bed is finished in luminous mother-of-pearl; the walls are covered in lustrous faux alligator; the gilt-framed mirror hangs above a mahogany-and-parchment dresser adorned by a well-polished sterling-silver flowerpot; and the bronze-based occasional table beside the reading chair is topped with an exquisite amethyst-colored glass. It's a space that makes you feel well taken care of in the highest of understated style—the decorative equivalent of arriving at your hotel in a chauffer-driven Daimler and sipping champagne while the valet unpacks your bags. Zen? Probably not. Soothing? *Definitely.*

Ultimately, a soothing abode is one that makes its residents feel special, and to me that's important. If you feel loved by your home, if it's a refuge in which you can enjoy the company of friends and compile happy familial memories, you'll return that good will to the world. A soothing home doesn't just welcome you in—it enables you, I firmly believe, to be the best person you can be. What could be more valuable than that?

PREVIOUS PAGE: A four-poster bed finished in mother-of-pearl, a coraline lamp, and an intricately woven silk-and-cotton cover create a bedchamber of serene elegance. OPPOSITE AND ABOVE: A mahogany-and-ivory parchment dresser and the gilt mirror and chair bring glamour into the same space.

In the absence of multiple colors and patterns, a range of intriguing textures quietly invigorates a relaxing space

My client's request for a bedroom finished in multiple shades of cream made the need for texture especially significant—hence such elements as the hemp-and-silk rug (OPPOSITE) and a faux-alligator wallpaper (RIGHT) that I had pearlized to bring in luster and dimension. The pale-pink lampshade (RIGHT) and amethyst glass tabletop (OPPOSITE) add a blush of color that's highly appropriate for so feminine a room, and the organic brass candlestick plays nicely off the angular architecture and furnishings.

You can be cosseted by your office—and still get the work done

OPPOSITE: I wanted my office to be at once feminine, business-like, and lighthearted—in other words, all me. Silk ruffle-trimmed curtains and curvilinear Louis XVI chairs address the first; a custom-designed Lucite desk and upholstered swivel chair (DETAIL ABOVE) speak to the second; and photos of Barbie and Ken living the good life take care of the third.

In most homes, the most soothing spaces are the bedrooms, which is why I try to avoid putting desks in them: They're objects that remind us of work. But what about the room in which a desk's presence is virtually unavoidable— the office? Is there a way to feel soothed in the space where we do our jobs?

I think so, though as with all such spaces, the conditions that create that relaxed, comfortable feeling remain highly individual. In my own office, three principal gambits did the trick. The first reverses my injunction against office furniture in private quarters: As it's the space in which I feel most soothed, I designed my office to resemble a feminine bedroom, with plush curtains, shimmering wallpaper, and carpeting that feels cozy under my feet. Some people might find it too intimate an environment for doing business, but I'm at my best in my ideal surroundings. And why should your office have to conform to someone else's notion of propriety?

The next step was to add personal elements—photos of my children, and objects that belonged to my parents and grandparents. They're just little things, but they ground me emotionally by reminding me of who I am and where I come from, in every sense. I try to have fresh flowers as well—a luxury, but since my job is to create beauty, it helps to have a bit of natural inspiration.

Lastly, I set the bulletin boards on which I pin up fabrics, photos, and sketches relating to projects in which the office is engaged on the walls where I can best see them. Most people don't realize this, but only about 20 percent of an interior designer's job is design—the rest involves meetings, logistics, management, and the like. My so-called "mood boards" represent the part of the work I most enjoy—so when I look up from my desk and see those pinups, I'm reminded of how lucky I am to have a job that I love, and of what a great gift that is.

Nothing could be more soothing —even if I am at work.

My high school's crest featured a snail above the legend *Festina Lente*—"Make Haste Slowly." When you're a teenager, that's difficult advice to accept, but now I appreciate the value of pausing to savor life's abundance, and my office, with its personal keepsakes and objects (OPPOSITE), reflects that.

Charm and serenity derive from soft colors distributed among patterns and objects

I love the unexpected combination of lavender and chartreuse, and paired them in multiple ways in my office: The fauteuils (ABOVE RIGHT) are upholstered in green leather with a more traditional purple damask on the back, and the chartreuse curtains (LEFT) feature lavender piping. The links of a favorite piece of jewelry inspired my custom-designed nickel-finished Sabina lantern (ABOVE LEFT). OPPOSITE: I filled my grandmother's candy jar with diet-friendly green marbles, and set it beside a vintage 1940s paperweight.

Soft, serene hues impart their own special magic— especially in a bedchamber

OPPOSITE: In my own bedroom, I balanced the shimmer of the ruched silk canopy interior with a matte-finished linen on the outside. Texture, sparkle, and sheen enliven the room without diminishing its welcoming serenity.

I f there's an overarching notion that drives my bedroom designs, it's that it is essential to have a place to quiet the mind and soul. I have said that different rooms should speak to different facets of one's personality, and many are devoted to being joyful, exuberant, and social. But most of us lead full, occasionally hectic lives, and at the end of the day, the room to which we retire should encourage us—indeed, make it possible—to put the hubbub aside and enjoy some peace.

My own bedroom represents a perhaps unexpected study in contrasts. No surprise—I want to feel warm, cozy, and cosseted, and certain of my choices address that: the selection of a clotted-cream color for the walls, to capture and embellish the rich infusions of natural light; a queenly canopy bed with an upholstered headboard and lush, enveloping linens. Yet the room also has a spare, architectural quality, with carefully chosen accessories that promote an atmosphere of meditative intimacy, a mood more appropriate to early mornings and late nights. Appropriately, my living room is abundantly layered, but the bedroom space required thoughtful editing.

One glance at the pages of this book, and you know I'm not a minimalist—when it comes to design, I am all for choosing self-expression over self-denial. But bedrooms demand restraint. They bring a degree of delicacy and intimacy to the great abundance of our days.

The mahogany Queen Anne dresser pictured above arrived as a gift from my husband's grandmother—and the print above it, by the contemporary artist Lisa Yuskavage, creates an effective counterbalance (and is one of my favorite pieces). OPPOSITE: I found the "Mozart" collage at an art fair. The jewelry drawers in my custom-designed shagreen-and-hammered-nickel dresser are lined with purple velvet, an indulgence that I adore.

My bedroom contains all of the elements I adore—color, sparkle, art, and texture—but all rendered in a muted tone

Floral aromas and decorative motifs— plus enchanting shades of lilac—make this corner of my bathroom a garden of earthly delights

For my husband's sake, most of our master bath is crisp, white, and spalike—thassos marble, subway tile, and nickel fixtures. But my little lilac corner (OPPOSITE), with its exquisite Manuel Canovas floral-patterned wallpaper, is my gift to myself; the fragrant soaps (ABOVE) and candles that I light when I settle into the tub at day's end evoke the aromas of a garden. While bathrooms aren't spaces in which we consider spending a lot of time, they can, if properly done, be among the most enjoyable rooms in one's home.

Although they require different considerations—durability and functionality uppermost among them—I've never believed that children's rooms should be infantilizing spaces that kids rapidly outgrow. Instead, I try to design bedrooms that are attractive and inspiring—interiors that children can grow *into*. This girl's room (OPPOSITE) is a good example: The wallpaper (ABOVE LEFT), crisscrossed with ribbons, is magnetic, so that she can pin up her artwork without making holes, and the shade I made from a soft, sophisticated pink satin, not a bubblegum color. But I didn't get *too* grown up: The big puff-ball chandelier (ABOVE RIGHT) was constructed from cut-paper flowers.

Perhaps more than any other color (with the exception of green), blue arrives at the eye carrying a set of natural associations that contrive to make it soothing: the sky; the sea; indeed, even light itself. Blue is cheerful—it reaches its arms out to the natural world, and brings the outdoors in. Who doesn't love blue?

Well . . . me. A little. It's not that blue hues give me the boo-hoos. But for a designer, blue can be too easy a choice—precisely because so many clients are blueheads. Which also means that the "wrong" blue can turn up with disheartening regularity—sweet blues that drift into the insipid. The challenge is to maintain blue's genuinely soothing, welcoming properties without letting it succumb to cliché—to give it resonance and originality.

So how do I do blue? I think carefully about the shades to which I respond most readily— periwinkle, cornflower, and cobalt—and the reasons why they speak to me, the better to use them to their optimum advantage. I appreciate periwinkle, for example, for its low notes of purple lavender—it's warmer, less minty than many default blues.

It can be effective as well to deploy small amounts of blue throughout a space—in elements of a painting, the patterns of a fabric, the decorative glaze of a ceramic bowl. Because it is a "friendly" color, the interplay between those bits of cheer, varying in shade, finish, and degree, can vitalize a scheme without subtracting from its soothing properties—indeed, the two are complementary, not incompatible.

The need to handle blue with consideration serves another important function: it reminds me that, for a design to be successful, every element requires my closest attention.

OPPOSITE: I try to combine different shades of blue—if I can create a tableau incorporating variations of the color in the walls, curtains, artworks, furnishings, and fixtures, I can achieve a uniqueness of character that might otherwise have gone unrealized.

The diversity of patterns in this beach-house living room—in the artworks, wallpaper, objects, and especially the throw pillows—brings the space subtly but distinctively to life.

Stripes, circles, and hexagons—thanks to varying shades of blue—prove to be complementary rather than combative

I've found blue to be a useful color if I plan to introduce strong graphic elements into a space. Or, to be more specific, *blues*: Variations in shade, intensity, and hue enable me to combine patterns that otherwise might seem incompatible—for example, the polka-dot abstract painting and striped wing chair, flanked by hexagon-patterned curtains (ABOVE). OPPOSITE: White-painted Chippendale-style chairs with leather cushions and a zinc-topped table with a wooden-cross base provide a lively interplay of materials and forms.

The light turquoise accents and silvered elements in this Manhattan living room imbue the largely monochromatic space with a serene sparkle—a perfect stage for the dramatic photographs of the Victoria and Iguazu Falls by Olivo Barbieri.

THE PAINTINGS OF BOB KANE: PEOPLE and PLACES

SLIM AARONS · ONCE UPON A TIME

TH AFRICA   *Michael Holland & Friends*

This room, which appears to have been designed in a single shade of blue (in fact there are subtle differences), is exceptionally soothing—but not boring, thanks to a wealth of texture. OPPOSITE: The wallpaper features a crosshatch pattern; the headboard is tufted and, like the armchair, upholstered in a glazed linen. ABOVE: A soft mohair blanket lies across the bed, and I shirred the fabric on the lampshades. Patterned curtains, shams, and pillows and the bordered mirror also fuel the space's undercurrent of energy.

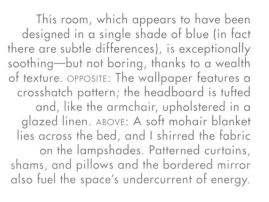

*Multiple textures
and quiet patterning
enliven a periwinkle
bedroom without
sacrificing serenity*

When it's suggested to me that certain of my color combinations—for example, purple and orange, which you'll see on page 118—are improbable or even jarring, I'll often seek evidence in the out-of-doors: Nature does purple and orange in the fall and pulls it off quite nicely, don't you think? But nature also does neutrals very well, and in a way that I find especially seductive. Think about the objects you can't resist gathering when you walk on the beach—a starfish, a bit of coral, some driftwood, shells. When you get them home, wash off the sand, and set them on the kitchen counter, they look great together—not only because their shades are so similar, but because we retain the memory of their irresistibly touchable textures in our hands. The fact is, we don't just *see* a palette composed of "natural neutrals"—with surprising immediacy, we *feel* it as well.

These tactile properties came strongly into play in this beach house dining room. I selected every element in the room with such pleasure: the cerused oak klismos chairs with their palpable grain, the rough raffia wall covering (painted with a coral motif), the thick sisal underfoot—even tabletop elements like the wood-handled flatware and specially glazed leaf-shaped plates. I always enjoy assembling the building blocks of an interior. But maybe it was even more fun in this instance, as everything felt so wonderfully appealing to the touch.

To my mind, the gentle caress of nature—whether in an interior or in life—remains one of the most deeply gratifying of experiences. The textures the natural world provided to this space lent it depth, warmth, approachability, and interest—and you couldn't keep your hands off it.

OPPOSITE: Stating the obvious is tricky, but if it is properly done, the effect can be surprisingly satisfying. Putting coral on the mantelpiece of a beach-house dining room might seem like a one-liner, but because there are abstracted coral motifs stenciled on the wallpaper behind it, the outcome is an unexpected dimensionality.

Natural objects, neutral tones: soothing to both the hand and the eye

OPPOSITE: An overscale oak table surrounded by cerused oak chairs serves as a perfect scene for lively family gatherings. I covered a brass chandelier with white plaster to make it less casual and more sculptural.

The *Magic* of the Mix

Masculine and feminine, shiny and matte, antique and modern, all create a delightful dynamism— who says opposites don't attract?

My mother isn't a decorator, but she's been a big influence on my professional style—because I grew up in rooms that were a delightfully unapologetic mishmash of all the things Mum accumulated and inherited. When I began my career, most interior designers took the opposite approach: rooms tended to be entirely faithful to a period—furnishings, artworks, and objects were all "correct." But because my mother had been "eclectic" before it was all the rage, when I started to design, I realized I'd picked up her perspective. Of course, there's a thoughtfully arrived at controlling idea undergirding all my schemes, and floor and furniture plans to reinforce it. But I still believe in embracing what you love and throwing it all in—there's magic in the mix.

As you can see from my dining room, I practice what I preach. It's a repository of all the lovely, cherished things I got from my grandmother—candelabras, china, saltcellars, a Wedgwood urn that evokes memories of what a gracious, generous woman she was. I've even got her gilt-framed portrait on the wall. That's a throwback to a bygone age, I know, but I love having her company at my dinner parties—and I always make it clear, as she did, that her fingers weren't actually that fat.

At the same time, the room also reflects my own, more contemporary tastes, notably in the choice of artworks—a pair of exquisitely lacquered blue disks by Justen Ladda—and the clean-lined modern dining table. The color scheme, too, is very much mine: walls with a Venetian plaster tinted a paper-bag brown, and lavender, lavender everywhere—in the glassware, upholstery, even the candles in Grandmother's ornate candelabra.

So many of my clients say, "I've got all this stuff that *isn't me.*" But I think you can reupholster, repurpose, and reinvigorate beloved old things and mix them up with the ones that *are* you, to produce richer, more resonant interiors. Look at it this way: If you yourself are interesting because you've got many different sides, shouldn't your home be as well?

OPPOSITE: The mirror above the fireplace in my dining room and the tilt-top Regency tray table before the hearth—both from my family—share an almost identical size and shape. ABOVE: The gilded stag's-head wall brackets that support my grandmother's plates are from the Evangeline Bruce estate, the source of several of my favorite treasures.

Objects needn't be new, or complementary, or even reflective of one's taste, to keep company—an abundance of beauty is its own reason for being

Among the family treasures that grace my table are antique candlesticks updated with purple tapers (LEFT), and a "plate tower" for serving desserts—I call it my cookie high-rise (BELOW LEFT). OPPOSITE: This nineteenth-century bronze-trimmed Wedgewood urn, from my grandmother's collection, reminds me that things we think of as "old-lady" can be both exquisite and timeless.

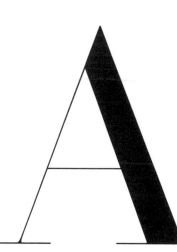

An important—crucial—part of the mix involves not objects but an element: *light*. It's a bit of a cliché to say so, but one of the truest maxims of the decorator's craft is that if a room isn't properly lit, it doesn't matter what's in it—it'll fall flat.

When I'm remodeling a residence, or building one from the ground up, one of the first things I'll give an architect or contractor is a lighting plan—it's that significant. So many aspects require consideration: overhead and art illumination, the placement of switches and dimmers, and, beyond the built-in fixtures, the selection and placement of task and reading lights. I also use light to apportion space: You can "zone" a room with atmospheric illumination as effectively as you can with furniture.

I've said that I always begin by finding the perfect object, one that sums up everything I want a project to express. Oftentimes this will prove to be a ceiling fixture—because a magnificent chandelier (from any period) can be a work of art in itself. Typically when we think about vintage pieces, it's furniture that comes to mind. Yet many of the design houses of legend—Bagues, Fontana Arte, Hansen, Kovacs, and Venini, to cite just a few—produced museum-quality lighting objects that rival the work of the finest *ebanistes*.

Indeed, if you want to see just how big an impact the right fixtures can have, pay a visit to the Boschi di Stefano house museum in Milan. Piero Portaluppi's interior architecture remains the acme of prewar modern elegance, and the walls are hung floor to ceiling with one of the most important art collections in Italy—but as you wander the rooms, it's the incomparable Venetian chandeliers that invariably command the eye.

In a dining room with a fourteen-foot-high ceiling, I needed an object that could occupy the vast spatial middle ground between the uppermost plane and the table. Tom Dixon's contemporary pendant fixtures make the dining area feel more intimate, and contrasts nicely with the room's traditional architecture.

A Hervé van der Straeten pendant (ABOVE LEFT) brings texture, sparkle, and movement—everything I value in a lighting fixture—to my front hallway. An orange scalloped trim enlivens a gray satin curtain in the same space (ABOVE RIGHT). OPPOSITE: My entryway contains a welcoming mix of objects and styles—a marble console, satin curtains, an antelope carpet, and Chinese porcelain vases.

No one likes to come upon a bug in a powder room, which is why I find this agate-and-brass critter so amusing. OPPOSITE: In another powder room, an agate sink, lit from within, brings a bit of Vegas to Manhattan's Upper East Side.

In the dining room of this New York apartment, I wanted to create a space elegant enough for a dinner party and practical enough for serving family breakfasts. The contemporary Sputnik lighting fixture sets a chic tone, and Lucite chairs with faux-shagreen upholstery support the mood.

One of the most effective ways of vitalizing a room is to introduce a note of contrast. Consider this kitchen: Into a rectilinear, glossily lacquered all-white space, with an overwhelming urban view, I introduced a row of Cherner bar stools—suavely organic in shape, the rich grain of their wood evocative of the (otherwise absent) pleasures of nature.

But another, more unexpected—and perhaps riskier—way of creating contrast is to bring into an otherwise well-judged space an element that's so outré or vulgar or downright ugly, it's, well, fabulous. A few pages back you'll find a pair of powder rooms that might fall into the LBV (Little Bit Vegas) category. The one on the left is part of a clean, minimalist New York apartment that, candidly, needed a jolt of levity. So I found this brass and agate bug that I couldn't resist—this funny little guy with weird eyes and long antennae—and stuck him in a corner of the loo: when you walk into the dimly lit space, there's nothing there but him. Apart from the kitschy aspects of the moment, I love the irony: the one thing you most definitely *don't* want to encounter in a Manhattan bathroom is a bug—and here's a great big backlit one staring right at you.

Such gestures can have a droll editorial quality, as with the second powder room, in which I inserted a slightly psychedelic agate sink that's lit from within. It is in an exceptionally tasteful, elegant apartment, the ideal setting for an intimate dinner party peopled by smart, sophisticated guests; and I imagined one of the diners excusing herself, visiting the loo, and silently screaming, "I can't take this another minute—I need a little Vegas *right now!*" That jazzy sink is your respite from all the civility: It gives you permission to hide, go a little crazy, and not be so proper.

I love designing little tongue-in-cheek moments like these. Just because something's beautiful and in the best of taste doesn't mean it can't—and shouldn't—be fun.

PREVIOUS PAGE: Softly undulating candlesticks (also above) by the designer Stephen Antonson sit atop the dining table, which is on the other side of the kitchen at right. The mix of machined and craft elements is one I always appreciate.

I believe it's important to treat hallways as though they were rooms—we spend much more time in them than we realize. In the long cross-axial halls of this New York City apartment, I finished the walls in a deep navy, textured-vinyl wallpaper. I conceived of the apartment as Manhattan in miniature—and these corridors are its dark, glamorous streets.

This child's bedroom, in a weekend home on New York's Long Island, had to do double duty as an occasional guest room. The design—its strongly graphic patterns realized in a crisp blue and white, with nickel accents—I characterize as masculine but beach-appropriate.

In a beach-house dining room, I hung a chandelier by Marjorie Skouras constructed of vibrant turquoise beads. My clients thought at first that it was too big for the space—then found that they enjoyed it as the culminating event in a room that is one big undulation.

Do you know René Magritte's iconic 1952 painting, *The Listening Room*? It's the one with the huge green apple that almost completely fills a small, otherwise entirely empty room. It really turns your head around, doesn't it? On the one hand, it's a deadpan visual joke. And on the other hand, there's something slightly menacing about how an ordinarily pleasurable edible has inflated to gargantuan proportions and entirely taken over the space. That mixture of drollery and menace is what makes the canvas exciting—and similarly unexpected alterations of scale can have a comparable effect in a room.

When I first proposed hanging a beaded turquoise chandelier in their beach house dining room, my clients balked—they thought it was much too big for the dimensions of the space. Perhaps—but it's also the culminating event in a room that's all about undulating, curvilinear shapes. Walk in, and the place almost seems to be ablaze, decoratively speaking, with the writhing chair backs forming the lower tier of flame, and the strongly patterned ikat curtains licking upward toward the ceiling. Given the context, having a big cloud of turquoise "smoke" suspended over the table is entirely appropriate—it's the perfect setting for an exuberant dinner party, at which the conversation's as fiery as the décor.

The crowning touch: the very cool, slick-surfaced seascape hanging behind the head of the table, like a very calm guest at a very raucous affair. I think Magritte would have approved.

OPPOSITE: Patinated-wood dining chairs beneath glamorous turquoise beads, energetic ikat curtains balanced by a serene seascape by photographer Tria Giovan, the luminosity of the tableware, and the roughly textured raffia window shades—it all adds up to quite a day at the beach.

This two-tiered living room, in a townhouse on Manhattan's Upper East Side, sums up all of my beliefs regarding the benefits of decorative bricolage. A big, overstuffed modern sectional sofa, on which the family's four children can sprawl in utter comfort, contrasts with more tightly tailored traditional armchairs. Two overscaled leaf-form chandeliers, executed in patinated metal, hang pendulously over the sitting areas and restate the lush tree forms in the garden outside the bay window. A resin-finished papier-mâché "rock" side table, which might have come from the estate of Fred and Wilma Flintstone, injects a moment of humor.

The dominant colors—blue, yellow, and malachite—forcefully hold their ground while also meeting in a mutually respectful truce. Three major patterns—in the sofa pillows, the carpets, and the upholstery on the fauteuil—suggest different periods but remain united by their strongly graphic qualities. An occasional table made of tubular steel members makes a crisp architectural statement within the sumptuous surroundings.

The room remains at once modern and traditional, elegant and functional, glamorous and down-home. It's a mix that, at bottom, is comfortable, welcoming, and consoling, without subtracting style or sophistication—properties that are paramount in all of my designs.

OPPOSITE: The armchairs in this living room originally combined a pale oak finish with a worn red fabric; a coat of black lacquer on the wood and a striking malachite linen print restored the chairs to life. Textured boxes on the coffee table pick up the pattern from the rug. I love the movement, beneath the window, of Jed Johnson's fabric design.

The interior of the gray cerused-oak coffee table is notched, so that the shelf can be raised or lowered. I liked the metal chandelier, one of a pair in the two-tiered room, for the way in which it brings in the garden. A Miró from my clients' collection sits atop a primitive side table.

VELÁZQUEZ
VELÁZQUEZ

There are four boys in the family, and this sectional sofa enables them all to sprawl en masse—the one spot in the room where the kids can gather. A strategically placed fern picks up the chandelier's drooping-leaf motif.

Books shown:
ARABIAN NIGHTS · CHAGALL
HERB RITTS PICTURES
THE END MONTAUK, N.Y. MICHAEL DWECK
The Great Book of French Impressionism

A Stone Age table, a hungry frog—such whimsical elements can make even the most proper room feel welcoming

OPPOSITE: I know: What's the deal with that frog? I found him in the family's kitchen and thought he was too much fun, and too funny, to be kept so far away from the main action. So I placed him next to a very proper chaise upholstered in a sophisticated cotton-and-silk damask—and gave him his own spotlight.

Pattern *Play*

Bold patterns can upend convention, reinvigorate tradition, and surprise and delight the eye

The caramel tones of the traditional wood paneling and the pink-and-white Positano fabric from my textile collection set the tone for this Kips Bay Show House room. As the Fauvist pattern makes such a strong impression, infusing the room with joie de vivre, I contrasted it with a softer palette.

P eople are often shocked by the ways in which I combine patterns. But the truth is, my approach is simply a contemporary version of what designers like Nancy Lancaster and Sister Parish did in the past. The traditional application, broadly speaking, involved swathing a room in a lovely chintz or toile, and complementing it with a gingham check; the combination of the energetic, free-flowing floral fabric and the crisp lines of the geometric print was at once stylishly fresh and enduringly timeless. I think it's a great formula—but why not reinvigorate it for the twenty-first century?

The bedroom I designed for the venerable Kips Bay Show House on Manhattan's Upper East Side gave me the perfect opportunity to do just that. I loved the restrained architectural elegance of the room's classical boiserie, the modesty of the carved fireplace contrasted with the overscaled French windows. Luckily for me, the other participating designers ran away from the space, precisely because its traditional qualities seemed insurmountable—they couldn't imagine applying anything other than a toile or chintz, and that felt too "old lady." I wanted to demonstrate that the seemingly antiquated décor could be shot through with modernity—that the old girl could be young again.

My custom-designed wall fabric—bold Fauvist strokes of hot pink on a white background—might at a glance seem wildly inappropriate. Yet to me, pairing it with the restrained traditional boiserie produced a perfect couple, a decorative portrait of the sort of society pair you see stepping into a taxi on Park Avenue after dark: an elegant, old-school gentleman with a vivacious woman on his arm. The combination's not inappropriate—it's life on the upper-crust Upper East Side as it's lived today.

ABOVE: The black base of this table grounds the room, and its clean lines contrast with all the surrounding movement. OPPOSITE: Eve Kaplan's mirror—hand-formed ceramic "rocks" painted in different shades of gold—reinterprets a traditional Regency design in a contemporary idiom, and contrasts appealingly with the nineteenth-century urn of gilt brass and marble.

It was important to me to give this room an edge, so I hung several contemporary artworks by Will Cotton and Marilyn Minter, intended to remind visitors that bedrooms aren't just for snoozing out over the *Wall Street Journal*. I also superimposed my own face onto a copy of an eighteenth-century nude by Watteau and Boucher: precisely the sort of canvas you would have found in the room a century ago, but with a cheeky twist.

The lively Fauvist wall upholstery pattern became languid and undulant when it moved to the furnishings and carpet

I wanted the colors of the wall upholstery and woodwork to look as though they'd slid down to the floor and formed large biomorphic puddles—hence the design of the ponyskin rug.

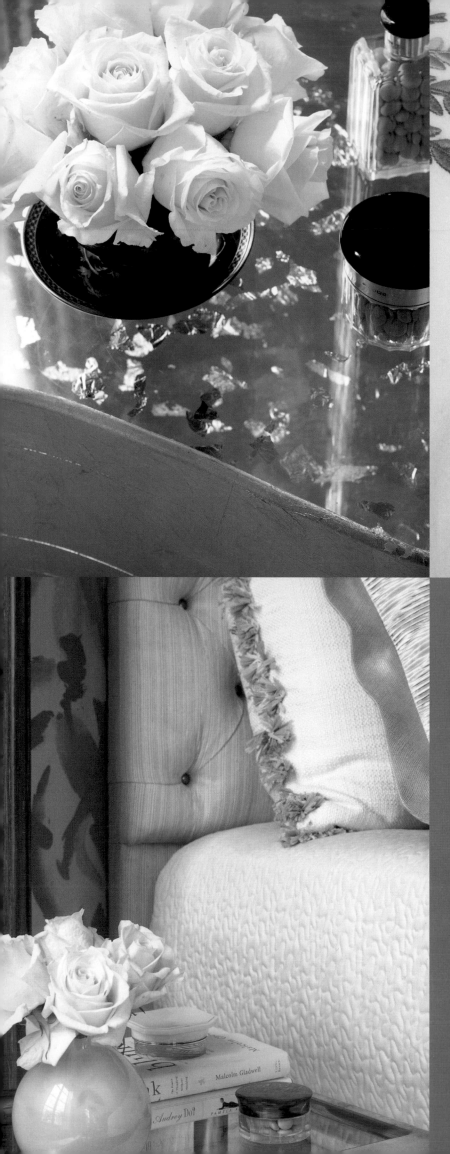

Pattern play can derive not only from mixing fabrics, but from contrasting elements—architectural, decorative, even organic

It's all in the details: A custom Lucite table of my own design with flecks of 24-carat gold leaf (ABOVE LEFT); pink embroidery on my line of linens (ABOVE RIGHT); and gold-leaf tassels and trim on pillows (LEFT). OPPOSITE: I love Lucite for both its luminosity and its modernity. Here, the contrast of the stand with a rustic urn makes the latter more graceful and light-seeming.

The strong graphic patterns appearing on fabrics and furnishings receive an impressionistic treatment in artworks

OPPOSITE: In a guest room in a beach house in Quogue, on Long Island, the leaf pattern on the blue-and-white headboards repeats in the punched openings in the night table shared by the twin beds.

A

s a rule, I don't believe in rules—except when it comes to mixing patterns. In that case, I scrupulously observe three tenets pertaining to scale, movement, and hue. *One:* The two principal patterns in a room should differ in scale—one larger, one smaller. *Two:* Select patterns with opposing movement, for example, the classic combination of a fluid toile and a geometric check. *Three:* Choose patterns in colors of a similar hue—a very strong, saturated shade next to a pastel won't work.

My application of the rules in this beach-house guest room is evident: The light fixture, bolsters, and window shades feature a large, undulating floral motif, while the slipper chair is covered in discreet squares; the colors—identical in temperature—differ sufficiently to liven each other up but not so much so that they raise eyebrows. And though it doesn't count as a rule, extending the dominant patterns to a room's other features—in this case the artworks and navy-stained cerused oak dresser—makes the space more cohesive and dynamic without subtracting from its tranquility.

As my decision to follow the rules suggests, manipulating patterns effectively remains a bit of a high-wire act and requires as much of a trained eye as does choosing colors. But when properly handled, patterns can inject vitality and visual interest into a space in delightful ways. Not least, "pattern play" is an excellent way to bring a thoughtful design sensibility to spaces that might otherwise be afterthoughts, like guest rooms—and, as you'll see when you turn the page, hallways.

OPPOSITE: While we typically associate patterns with fabrics and rugs, organic materials such as wood have a natural patterning that can be enhanced and foregrounded. One of my favorite treatments in this regard is cerusing (TOP RIGHT)—the process of painting on, then wiping off, pigment to enhance the grain of oak.

Two different colors in a layered beach-
house hallway emphasize the architecture's
planar qualities. OPPOSITE: A fun yet
elegant graphic pattern enlivens the full
five floors of a townhouse stairwell.

This room was architecturally undistinguished, and my Alannah fabrics
and the furnishings I chose for it were simple and straightforward. But by
layering bold graphics patterns and objects with strong profiles against
a rich blue backdrop, I was able to make it unexpectedly elegant.

In my daughter's room, the Greek-key pattern in the carpet and headboard make this corner feel well crafted and cozy

In my daughter's room, the discreet chocolate-brown Greek-key motif in the rug (RIGHT) inflates to grand proportions in the headboard (ABOVE). OPPOSITE: The fabric on the bed and shades, a cozy cotton-linen blend that feels like velvet to the touch, mixes lavender and pink hues with a hint of fuchsia; combined with the smart navy trim, it feels at once contemporary and classical. In keeping with my belief that children should grow into, rather than out of, their rooms, the artworks are whimsical but not childish.

Even casual spaces like kitchens should be treated with care and attention—the patterns in the flowerpot, candlesticks, and window shade add an overlay of elegance

OPPOSITE: To bring some glamour into the room, I repurposed a polished mahogany and metal desk and made it into my kitchen table, but sliding comfortably onto the banquette is impossible—another design lesson learned the hard way. The table works beautifully with the green leather and steel chairs, though; sometimes you have to suffer for style.

A consistency of color serves as
a discreet and supportive partner
to repeating patterns and motifs

There's *always* Snow in
Stowe
VERMONT

PAINTING IN RENAISSANCE FLORENCE

ITALIAN RENAISSANCE ART

La Vilaine Lulu

CALATRAVA

In my son's room, I framed his orange headboard in a link-print border, a pairing that
plays out elsewhere in the room: The same
border turns up on the orange curtains. One of
the two prints I hung on the wall received an
orange matte; for the other I used the link-print
fabric. My son, Travers, made the ceramic
dog in grade school. I'm passionate about
including children's artwork in my interiors.

When several bold prints take visual command of a space, it's logical to choose simple, soothing artworks, such as the black-and-white seascapes I hung in a bright-yellow, starburst-patterned stair hall. But what happens when you're working with images that are highly graphic—pictures that constitute patterns in and of themselves? How do you work a strong visual into a space in which patterns also play a part?

One solution, which I applied in my son's room, is to establish the same sort of relationship between the art and the other decorative elements as I would between two different fabrics. My son's sports posters, with their horses and skiers, convey a compelling sense of movement—the sort of sweep you might find in a lively floral-print wallpaper. So I contrasted them with smaller, more regular circle motifs, most evident in the geometric fabric on the bed's headboard, on throw pillows, and even on the mattes of the posters.

As in other of my patterned spaces, the colors in the posters and the room are closely related: russet, red, and brown, with a bit of gold for elegance and shimmer. The blue in the skiing poster pleasantly throws off the plan a bit—it gives the overall scheme a jolt of vitality.

Many, if not most, patterned rooms lean toward the feminine, but not this one—it possesses the sporty elegance one associates with an English gentlemen's club. I've said that a child's décor needn't be childish, and my son's room serves as a good example: It's maturing as nicely as he is.

OPPOSITE: The repeating circle motif in my son's room— which appears in the nailheads on the bedroom door (TOP LEFT), the link motif in the picture matte (BOTTOM LEFT), a pendant fixture (TOP RIGHT), and a table lamp (BOTTOM RIGHT)—is at once vitalizing and calming.

THE
TRAVERS
127th Running

Saratoga 1996

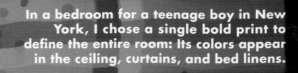

In a bedroom for a teenage boy in New York, I chose a single bold print to define the entire room: Its colors appear in the ceiling, curtains, and bed linens.

My ideas for a teenage boy's room included putting his initials above the bed, styled as a sophisticated double D—now he's got his own logo. The vividly patterned rug counterbalances the design's tight tailoring and rich masculine colors.

Humor and whimsy lend warmth and a personal touch to every kind of space—and play a welcome role in all of my designs

In a show-house bathroom, I added some witty touches: Shake Your Buddha towels (RIGHT), a spiky pink mirror (ABOVE) made from a street sweeper's brush, and my favorite—"You look marvelous" scrawled on the front of a chalkboard (OPPOSITE). I also included some personal objects, which reflects my feeling that such touchstones are essential to infusing a home with soul.

182

SHAKE YOUR BUDDHA

Terrific
Texture

You may not always be aware of its presence, but a well-designed room derives depth and dimension from layers of texture

W

hen we think about texture, the first word that comes to mind is touch. But texture can also refer to the appearance of an object or surface; the particular nature of a work of art (in any medium); or the hours and days of one's life. Texture in design is all of these things: the look and feel of the fabrics and finishes, the ways in which they shape the micro and macro of a particular interior, and most of all the means by which that interior influences the day-to-day experience of those who inhabit it. I've talked a lot about texture, and for a reason: In a sense, it's everything.

This room is a veritable cornucopia of texture. A layer of cutout paper rides over walls painted a peacock blue. Striations in the silk carpet caress the feet and catch the light. The nubby rubber lounge chair, which looks industrial, proves surprisingly cozy. The luminosity of the mouth-blown glass chandelier harmonizes with the glossily lacquered reflective ceiling above it. Even the rivulets of oil paint cascading down the Mel Bochner canvas above the sofa attract the hand. Thanks to texture, what otherwise might have been an atonal space ripples with variation—with dimension.

Dimension is key: It makes the difference between an experience that ends when it begins and one that's rich with possibility. A single-texture room—for instance, one done entirely in silk damask, cotton chintz, or heavy velvet—can certainly be beautiful. But I like there to be a conversation in a space—and if there's a sufficiency of texture, it can go on indefinitely.

OPPOSITE AND ABOVE: The strongly graphic edge of the adjustable shelving system I designed for the room contributes an additional layer of visual texture to the overall design scheme.

Though we typically associate texture with materials, reflective surfaces can add "virtual" texture to a space

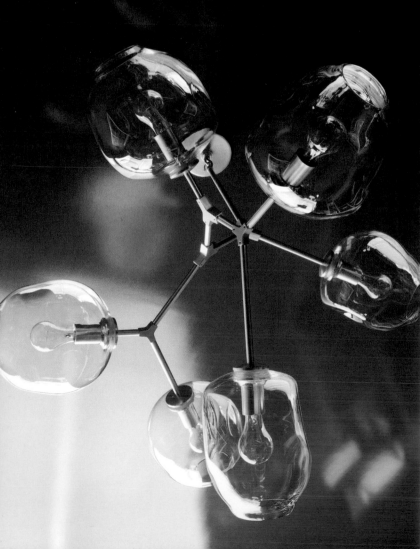

ABOVE: I painted the walls of this library a high-gloss peacock blue, then applied a wall treatment made from a cutout bark paper to combine color, pattern, and texture. My custom-designed "Travers" wall sconce bears my maiden name (Travers is also the middle name of both my children, a familial homage to George Foreman). LEFT: The mouth-blown glass chandelier is reflected in the lacquered ceiling. OPPOSITE: The blue in the glass boxes atop the 1960s-vintage coffee table echo the color's appearance elsewhere in the room.

188

One of the things I most enjoy doing is creating functional spaces that retain a quality of elegance. Fortunately, I'm practicing in the early twenty-first century, and my clients spend most of their time in the room typology that epitomizes our age: the combination kitchen/breakfast room/TV-watching area. Such spaces get a ton of use, and though each component wants its own personality, as they all intercommunicate, the elements demand a decorative connection. One of the most effective means of making that connection—and imbuing a functional, multiuse space with panache—is via texture.

In this particular room, for a Manhattan family with three children, I used an abundance of one of my favorite materials, gunmetal-gray cerused oak—in the kitchen cabinets, the base of the banquette, and the shelf behind the sofa—to create a unifying neutral ground. To complete the picture, I let the texture of the oak slip down to the comparably colored porcelain tile floor, where it appears as a more dimensional striation.

Once I established unity, I was able to use other textures (in combination with color) to introduce variations from zone to zone, most notably with the chartreuse faux-alligator patent leather on the banquette and check-patterned woven throw pillows on the sofa that bring in a brighter shade of green.

Here I've benefitted from the fact that the eye perceives texture differently than the hand. The oak, porcelain, and matte-finish painted walls all feel quite distinct, but we "read" them in a more uniform way. Together, they create order and calm in a busy, relatively confined collection of linked spaces—just the sort of functional elegance I always try to achieve.

OPPOSITE: The planar elements in this contemporary multiuse room vary materially but maintain a consistent color palette and lightly striated texture. On top of this neutral ground, woven leather chairs, a glass-topped table, nickel hardware, and globe-shaped chandeliers (NEXT PAGES) create discreet visual energy.

Maintaining a consistent texture in the background elements of this living/kitchen/TV room enabled me to maintain calm and consistency in a space that's busy both visually and programmatically.

The textures of organic elements—antlers, branches, animal hides—invite the presence of nature into even the most sophisticated room

OPPOSITE: I upholstered the walls of this family room in a gold-flecked gray velvet to give the space an enveloping texture; mohair-upholstered chairs and a cowhide rug add variation and interest. The unexpected purple silk fabric (ABOVE) that covers the sofa provides the room with a swoony, lustrous glamour.

Multipurpose family rooms come in many forms. Usually, we think of them as being unbuttoned spaces that mix kitchen and breakfast areas with a place to congregate in front of the television. Not this room. While the individuals inhabiting the house use it to read the paper, do homework, and enjoy casual meals, it's anything but casual in flavor. The architecture is quite grown up, and the proportions very grand—the ceiling rises to a height of fourteen feet. What's more, the space communicates directly with the house's dining room, so putting up a giant flat-screen and hanging sports memorabilia wasn't an option. The challenge was to make the room user-friendly and inviting while also giving it an overlay of sophistication suitable to the setting.

Texture provided the solution—by enabling me to create a mood. Consider a woman in a magnificent formal gown, or a gentleman wearing a bespoke tailored tux: There's something about the fine fabrics from which their clothes are made, I find, that captures the very essence of elegance. The best materials, which look and feel so sublime, emit a palpable sense of quality and style—and that's as true in the textures of a room as in a wardrobe.

For that reason, I upholstered the foot rests in the same buttery leather found on vintage Deco club chairs from the interwar years. The material provides an emotional cue—you think of the raffish chic of a Parisian parlor, a place to sip champagne with your feet up. The mood's reinforced by my choice of wall covering: gray velvet, flecked with gold. On the one hand, über-luxurious; on the other, as cozy as a lap robe on the deck of a transatlantic liner. Each material sends a double message: high style, casual comfort.

OPPOSITE: By carefully considering my selection of textures, I was able to take the starch out of this rather formal family room and make it comfortable and welcoming—which is what a space for a young, fun clan needs to be.

OPPOSITE: The value of making a glamorous entrance is evident in the front hall of this New York apartment. The dark graphite ceiling, lacquered to a high gloss, at once echoes and provides a counterpoint to the marble floor, in which narrow center slabs contrast directionally with the border (ABOVE RIGHT). Stephen Antonson's plaster-framed mirror (ABOVE LEFT) hangs on a wall finished in blue bark paper (LEFT).

My design for this four-poster bed—which is solid nickel—came out of pure creative frustration: I just couldn't bear the thought of doing my umpteenth upholstered headboard and wanted to come up with something completely original.

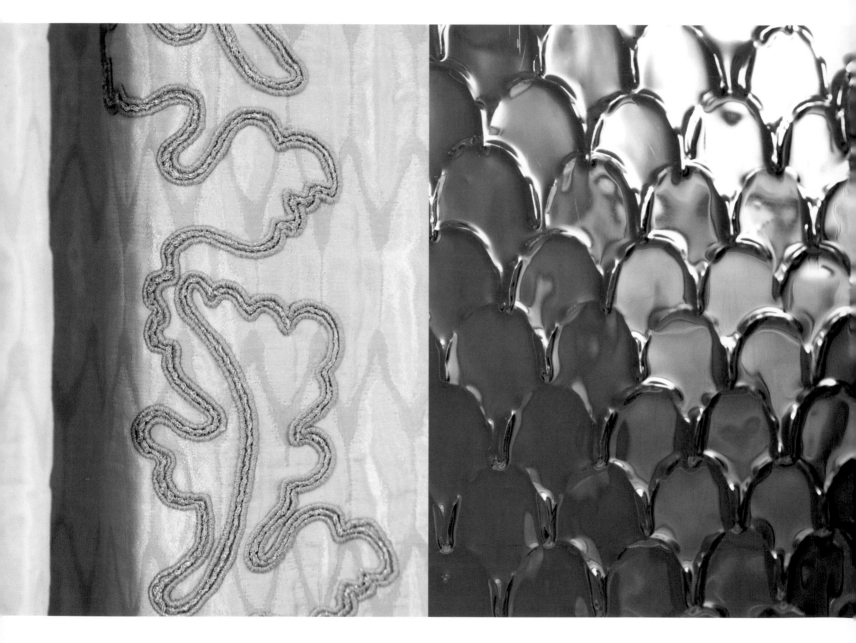

ABOVE LEFT: What might be described as "doctoring" preexisting elements can be an effective decorative gambit: Witness the visual interest and overlay of craft that derive from the thread pattern I wove into the curtains. ABOVE RIGHT: The fish-scale motif on the headboard creates texture while remaining crisp, clean, and simple. OPPOSITE: The bed's reflectivity also appears in the wallpaper, in a custom silver-and-blue color. The large-format photograph (of peeling paint) is by Frank Thiel.

OPPOSITE: I migrated the nickel from the bedroom to the adjacent bath, using it to trim the milk-glass drawers. Quatrefoil milk-glass floor tiles are interspersed with octagonal clear-glass inserts.

Burlap-wrapped shadowboxes, each displaying a single specimen of coral, transform texture into art

OPPOSITE: Wicker baskets, a sisal rug, chairs with woven-cane seats and backrests, unfinished wood, and one of my very favorite fabrics—burlap—combine to create this most touchable of environments.

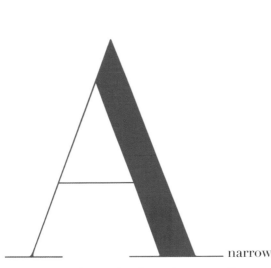A narrow wraparound porch—just the sort of space you *don't* want to get stuck with. But that's the booby prize I received when I was invited to participate in this Bridgehampton, Long Island, show house. Nonetheless, I hoped to make it not just inhabitable, but even a source of pleasure, the sort of perch from which you'd be happy to take in the abundance of country life. Fortunately the porch had a big built-in plus: What could be more inviting than the "found" texture of a shingled exterior wall?

I've always loved shingles, both for their rough, quotidian beauty and for their association with being out in the garden or by the seashore, with nothing more to worry about than whether to have lobster or steamers for supper. My job was to draw that feeling into a more formalized design scheme without losing its essence—a bit like capturing lightning in a bottle. Thinking it over, I hit upon the idea of creating arrangements of shadowboxes on the walls, but covering them with burlap, a fabric with much the same textural and associative appeal as shingles; the burlap enabled me to put art on the walls without making the porch feel overly civilized or, worse, precious. Finally, I mounted pieces of coral in the boxes—"artworks" that come by their sculptural sophistication naturally, and proved as appealing to the touch as the two layers of material behind them.

As you've surely intuited by now, I'm hooked on the ability of texture to evoke memories and emotions—it is one of the subtlest yet most powerful aesthetic weapons in a designer's arsenal—and my show-house porch offered me a singular opportunity to deploy it. You'll see it as well in the zinc-trimmed mirror I hung above a burlap-covered table, zinc being another kind of material code—for a bucket.

And that is how I turned my booby prize into a blue ribbon.

OPPOSITE: Patterned linen curtains make this porch feel less like a circulation space and more like an outdoor living room. An infusion of periwinkle brings out the texture in the wooden ceiling boards and the woven-raffia seat cushions.

While I wanted the porch to be as comfortable and habitable as a space inside, I didn't want it to lose its pleasurable connection to the out-of-doors. An abundance of flowers and plants serve as a reminder that being in the country is all about being out of the house.

I've talked a lot in these pages about the importance of fun and whimsy in interior design—about how not taking myself too seriously helps me to create residences that embrace life in all its colors, and nurture us so that when we go back out to engage with the world, we can do so with optimistic hearts and smiles on our faces (not to get too sappy about it).

That philosophy played a large role in the design of this room. You've undoubtedly guessed, from various of its materials and motifs, that it's a beach house, which raises an interesting question: How does one design a "themed" room that doesn't become kitschy or cute?

In my own view, the secret lies in one's intentions. Here we have a massive wooden coffee table—nearly seven feet in length—that with its organic form and softly sculpted edges recalls a big piece of driftwood that generations of beachgoers might have used as an ad-hoc picnic table. The wonderfully tongue-in-cheek braided rope stools are stand-ins for your beach bag—not only comfortable to sit on, but easy to pick up by the handle and carry from conversation to conversation. As for the sisal rug with its gentle wave pattern, it at once evokes the shifting striations of sand and the lines of foam left by the receding waves on the shore.

But the design (I hope) doesn't feel "theme-y" because my intention wasn't to pull together an ensemble of beach-going references of the sort you'd find in a seafood restaurant on a pier. Rather, I wanted my clients to be able to kick back in a stylish, comfortable setting that gave them the same keen pleasure they experience when they go off, for the day, to the sea. I wanted them to have fun—to always be reminded why they wanted a beach house in the first place.

Whether I'm working with texture, color, pattern, or a great mix-up of all three, the objective is always the same: to create a sense of joy, approachability, and grace. Life is for living—and design is for living *in*.

OPPOSITE: Though many of the elements in this beach-house living room explicitly evoke the sea, I wanted the space to retain a certain in-town sophistication. Accordingly, while the sofa is upholstered in a sturdy blue linen, tufting the fabric lends an overlay of elegance. The décor also reinforces a curious but dependable interior-design maxim: The more furniture you put in a room, the bigger it looks.

A sensuous abstract watercolor by the artist Ray Kass captures the presence of the sea for me. Combining it with mounted fossilized ocean creatures and a lovely, natural-wood console table with a bow front and serpentine legs enabled me to create a tableau that's both lively and delicate and plays off the blue in the upholstery and curtains (OPPOSITE).

Structural columns are the curse of modern construction, and coming up with creative ways to get around them can be challenging. Here I chose to embrace the obstacle, by wrapping it in a wallpaper with a pattern of thousands of faces (I'll bet the boy whose room this is has added a few of his own).

This room's elements represent an appealing balance of color, texture, craft, pattern, and history. The dresser's unusual design (ABOVE LEFT) recalls a casually stacked series of boxes. OPPOSITE: The custom carpet (LEFT) was stitched together from multiple panels of blue felt; Arne Jacobsen's Egg chair (RIGHT) reminds me of everything I love about great and timeless design.

Resources

Albert Menin Interiors, Ltd.
www.albertmenin.com

Amy Merrick Flowers
    & Styling
amy@amymerrick.com

Beauvais Carpets
www.beauvaiscarpets.com

Bergamo & Donghia
www.bergamofabrics.com

Bermingham and Co.
www.berminghamfabrics.com

Bob Kane
(212) 877-3057

Brunschwig & Fils
www.brunschwig.com

Caba Company
(505) 983-1942

Cadogan Tate
www.cadogantate.com

Carlos de la Puenta Antiques
www.delapuenteantiques.com

Chelsea Workroom
www.chelseaworkroom.com

Christopher Spitzmiller Inc.
www.christopherspitzmiller.com

Claremont Furnishing
    Fabrics Company
www.claremontfurnishing.com

Clarence House
www.clarencehouse.com

Cowtan & Tout
www.cowtan.com

Dinosaur Designs
www.dinosaurdesigns.com

Donzella Furniture
www.donzella.com

Duane
www.duaneantiques.com

Eddy Interiors and Dec. Inc.
(917) 837-0705

Edwina Hunt
www.edwinahunt.com

Eve Kaplan
kaplaneve@gmail.com

Fabricut
www.fabricut.com

Farrow & Ball
www.farrow-ball.com

Fedora Design
www.fedoradesign.com

Flair
www.flairhomecollection.com

Fortuny
www.fortuny.com

F. Schumacher
www.fschumacher.com

Gerald Bland
www.geraldblandinc.com

Harbinger
www.harbingerla.com

Holland & Sherry LTD
www.hollandandsherry.com

Holland Cunningham
(212) 289-7456

ILevel Art Placement
    and Installation
www.ilevel.biz

John Rosselli
www.johnrosselliantiques.com

John Salibello
www.johnsalibelloantiques.com

J. Pocker & Son
www.jpocker.com

Koroseal
www.koroseal.com

Kyle Bunting
www.kylebunting.com

Lars Bolander
www.larsbolander.com

Lauren Hwang, Inc.
www.laurenhwangbespoke.com

Lee Calicchio
www.leecalicchioltd.com

Leontine Linens
www.leontinelinens.com

Liz O'Brien
www.lizobrien.com

Louis Bofferding
(212) 744-6725

Luther Quintana Upholstery
www.lqupholstery.com

Mary Ryan Gallery
www.maryryangallery.com

Matter
www.mattermatters.com

Maya Romanoff
www.mayaromanoff.com

Mecox Gardens
www.mecoxgardens.com

Mitchell Studio, LLC
www.mitchellstudio.net

Moore and Giles
www.mooreandgiles.com

MZ Movers
www.mzmovers.com

Nanz Custom Hardware
www.nanz.com

Nathan A. Bernstein & Co.

Ltd.
www.nathanbernsteinart.com

Niermann Weeks
www.niermannweeks.com

Pace Prints
www.paceprints.com

Penn & Fletcher, Inc.
www.pennandfletcher.com

Phillip Jeffries LTD
www.phillipjeffries.com

Pierre Frey, Inc.
www.pierrefrey.com

Plexi-Craft
www.plexi-craft.com

Reynolds Gallery
www.reynoldsgallery.com

Robert Bristow
Poesis LLC
www.poesisdesign.com

Robert Massello Antiques
(646) 293-6633

The Rug Company
www.therugcompany.info

Samuel & Sons Passementerie
www.samuelandsons.com

Scalamandre
www.scalamandre.com

Sferra
www.sferra.com

Soane Britain
www.soane.co.uk

Staley Wise Gallery
www.staleywise.com

Stark Carpet Corporation
www.starkcarpet.com

Stephen Antonson
www.stephenantonson.com

Studio Four NYC
www.studiofournyc.com

T4
www.t4designs.com

Tigger Hall Design
www.tiggerhall.com

Travis & Company
www.travisandcompany.com

Treillage Ltd.
www.treillageonline.com

Two Palms Press
www.twopalms.us

The Urban Electric Company
www.urbanelectricco.com

Vaughan Designs, Inc
www.vaughandesigns.com

Acknowledgments

I owe a great debt of gratitude to my publisher, Stewart, Tabori & Chang, for believing in this book and giving me the opportunity to share my work—truly, a dream come true. Leslie Stoker, Dervla Kelly, and Wesley Royce thank you for your intelligence, perseverance, and wise counsel.

I am indebted to my agent, Jill Cohen, who helped me through every step of this process with true friendship and professionalism—thank you.

Doug Turshen, who designed the book, is a man of great artistic vision and blessedly even temperament—his talent, and Steve Turner's organizational abilities are evident on every page.

My jumbled thoughts and random musings have eloquently been put into articulate prose by the very intelligent, patient, and witty Marc Kristal.

All designers owe a great debt to the magazine editors who discover and publish their work, and I am no exception. I am so thankful for the encouragement I've received from Margot Austin, Jenny Bradley, Dara Caponigro, Kendell Cronstrom, Carolyn Englefield, Pamela Jaccarino, Jason Kontos, Ann Maine, Robert Rufino, Margaret Russell, Doretta Sperduto, and Newell Turner.

The *über*-talented photographers whom I've had the privilege to collaborate with over my career have all brought out the very best in my work. William Abranowicz, John Bessler, William Geddes, Tria Giovan, Stacey Haines, and my dear friends Max Kim-Bee and Roger Davies—thank you all.

I have had the great privilege of working with Sam Mitchell of Mitchell Studio and the affable Bill Pollack.

The mechanics of any design business are complicated, and I am lucky to have John Bryan, Bob Mass, and Tim Blanco to keep mine running smoothly. I am thrilled as well to be in partnership with the Urban Electric Co. and have Dave Dawson, Michael Amato, and Regina Martin to thank for supporting my creativity. Bryan Dicker of Holland and Sherry, Joe Lucas and Parrish Chilcoat of Harbinger: thank you for your appreciation of, and support for, AND textiles. My appreciation as well to Patrick McBride and Kathleen Tillett for your enthusiasm for helping to make AND textiles a reality. Christina Juarez: thank you for your charm, intelligence, and support.

None of my projects would have come to fruition without the hard work and dedication of everyone who has worked at AND: Anne Patterson, Lizzie Bailey, Leah Margolis, Lindsay Feldman, Alexis Manfer, Avery Leigh Cox, Heather Caster, Maggie Waltemath, Stephanie Henderson, and Raymond Schneider—a very special thanks to each and every one of you.

I am most grateful to the many clients who have entrusted me with the very intimate and special task of designing their homes. You have all become my dear friends, and have my utmost gratitude.

I grew up in a lovely home, in which life was enjoyed for everything it had to offer, and if my parents had not taught me to appreciate art, travel, and beauty, I doubt very much that I would have flourished in my profession. Thank you, Mum and Dad—I love you tons and owe all of my talents and good fortune to you. Thanks as well to my fabulous sister, Francesca, for her constant love, support, and friendship. Nicholas, Benjamin, Sabina, and Poppy: Your consistent love and cheerleading make me a very lucky aunt and sister-in-law.

Most of all, I thank my husband, Chip, who not only supports my career but gives me carte blanche to design and redesign our home. My children, Alannah and Travers, have put up with the rotating of furniture and art all their lives—and the "fun" of having a working mother. You are good-humored and patient with me—I love you.